Poetry for the Absence Vol.1

A philosophers dairy

By: Abel Conlget

Poetry for the Absence

Published by AE books, Fresno Ca

AE book logo are trademarks of AE inc

ISBN-13: 978-0-692-18523-0

ISBN-10: 0692185232

Series design by Conlget

Printed in the United states of America

Special thanks to:

Command Sargent Major Manis

First SGT Banogon

Blake Gibson

SSG Bluhm
Kevin Green

Taylor Baker

SSG Labonty

SSG Mateus

Rowe

Cain

Holland

Gallow

Savoy

SSG Salcedo

Sgt Ruble

Soldier X

Kersten

Doc Green

Doc Cook

Zochert C co.

Jordan Mckee C co.

Ryan Kelleher A co.

Causey B co.

Albert B co.

Zackary Gwin

The Omen element

2-27 Wolfhounds

No fear

And those who gave the ultimate sacrifice

Written and illustrated by: Abel Conlget

Edited by: Deborah Heimann

Table of Contents

This story is set with quotes and poems, numbered 5 through 1, as the letters to each number rises, that shows the gain of knowledge, as the numbers get smaller that brings you closer to the end.

5

4

3

2

1

0

Introduction

This poem book is an eight-year journey that is based on war and philosophy, and life after war. Each poem is unique and shares something new, dark, sad, and a journey to find happiness. These poems were written during the time I was in combat. They hold something very dear to me and my fellow brothers in arms. This is me paying back those close to me that did not make it. I still say this to myself: "gone but never forgotten." Each poem was selected to share what my life was during combat and the struggles after while trying to maintain my path to my end goal.

Chapter One

Blind Innocence

There I was, waiting for Bus #30 at 7am with warm winds at my face. I was going to my first Fresno City College class of the day, swim. Before I got on the bus I smoked the rest of my joint. After swim class, I had a few art classes, and before going I would smoke weed with my pals. I listened to the lecture of the day, about how to use different shades of a color to show emotions. I wanted to be a world artist, but the words of the professor echoed in my mind: "With an art degree you have a very high chance of teaching art. It is very unlikely that anyone here will make it as a world artist." After class, I did the only thing I could think of: I went to the Army recruiter.

We talked, and he told me that the most Army could offer me was more schooling, and they would pay for it. *What else have I got to lose?* I thought to myself, so I signed up. My Father was infantry, so I picked it, too. Might as well follow something.

5a

The self *"prison"* is only a
setback to one's *"freedom."*

2007–2009

All I knew was Fresno, smoking weed, women, and my friends, so it was hard leaving it behind.

By joining the military, and as an infantry man, I learned so much more then I could have ever thought. I was so dumb. I was a college guy, partying every day, and hanging out with any girl but now I ended up waking up at 5am, learning how to shoot, and work out, and how to fight, and push myself. In this world I was not the cool guy, not the tough dude. In basic, I had to run more than I had ever run and lift more than I had ever lifted. I had to learn to become tough, which I was not used to. This new world was something I did not belong in, but like everyone around me, I finished, and I passed, and I did it with a smile, my Basic company was Alpha 2-19, 3rd platoon.

We leave our old world and enter a new one, and sometimes it is very uncomfortable, but we know, if we can manage it, our next world will be better. It is ok to move forward and leave the old behind. It is ok to grow and not turn back.

5b

My conclusion is that an
end is only
a beginning. We are
"designed"
to move forward.

August 2010

I had been in the army for one year. I was with the 25th Division, 3rd Brigade, 2nd Battalion, 27th infantry the Wolfhounds, and like our forefathers, we partied, had fun, fought drunk among ourselves, and stood up for the guys to our left and right.

I left Hawaii and ended up in Afghanistan. I was the last one to meet my platoon in Kunar, Afghanistan. Alone, I sat on the chopper from Jabad (or FOB Fintie) to Bostic waiting for it to land at the place I, like many others before me, would call home. I was afraid, of course, but the chopper landed, and I got off. Huge mountains hugged my sights. I stood alone on the landing pad, thinking to myself, *so this is what us humans have been doing since the start of our time?*

What I was doing was not new, and though I was new to this life, that did not mean my soul was new to war.

Two folks from 4th ID we were taking over came up running to me, I told them my platoon, and they helped me bring my bags to my living quarters.

<u>5c</u>

An old soul born with a
new mind.......

April 2011

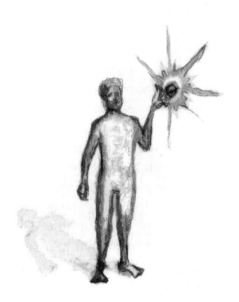

On the third day of the year, my team was on the shooting range when I heard new sound. Everything went in slow motion. I looked up and thought *Why is the chopper doing such a sharp turn?* I heard my platoon leader SSG Gibsion scream "GET DOWN!" I was still standing when he yanked on the front of my shirt and pulled me down. The pull was quick, it popped my neck. That sound got louder and louder. Then BOOM, I felt the shock wave hit us, and I heard my platoon leader scream again "RUN!" Each of my team had to run over a football length away and rounds fell around us, running through the sonic booms and falling rocks I was last to make it back.

Once I got to our barracks, everyone was laughing, joking with excitement, punching one another. I was pulled into the group and my weapon was taken away and I became part of the joke. Laughing at me, and with me. Our platoon leader came in, and his smile and laughter helped me calm down.

A new voice in me arose, a quiet one. I knew this year would be something hard to put into words, so I started a journal and this is it.

<u>5d</u>

I am a lost voice among
myself, I am
my *"keeper,"* the fire that
burns
my soul is set by me.

April 2011

Each month, the whole battalion, as a team, would get supplies—mail, ammo, fuel, and more. I remember sitting in the truck while my platoon sergeant was calling around for an energy drink. We had none. I was the driver. I looked through my night vision sights, seeing tracers shoot from mountains, then other tracers hitting those places, choppers flowing back and forth, waiting for someone to shoot at the supplies so they could hit them with rounds or rockets all while, Green, Salcedo and me talked of nonsense. From the distance it looked like fireworks. As the supply came by, I crunched on dirt from all the dust. I saw trucks with random colors and bells hanging from the sides of them.

When our task was done, we drove to Monti, which was Bravo's outpost. I got off to hang with my old pals from 1st platoon Bravo company. When we met a preacher, he prayed for us.

I watched him walk away and thought, *forever sounds bad, when this is the life we must live through.* I sat with 1st platoon Bastard company, folks made fun of me for being in PSD, but it was nice to be next to my pals, and I smiled too.

<u>4a</u>

The bitter test of eternal life

April 2011

Chapter **Two**

Kunar Afghanistan and Me

My team drove back to our OP, Bostic. It took one day and one night. A few times we would get a random pop shot, from snipers, trying to fish us in to a fight, but we drove through the night. We got to Alpha's OP, Pearl King, or PK, and as we drove in to the small entrance, one gunner opened fire just above our trucks. Sgt Salcedo was yelling, "Why the FUCK are they shooting over our trucks?" We thought they were test firing.

We were in the middle of a firefight. Rounds flew going both ways. As my gunner started to shoot up the mountains, Sgt Salcedo had to jump out and help me park the truck. I could see him running behind sand bags while giving me hand signals as tracers followed him. He jumped back in and told my gunner, Green, to stop shooting. He said this is not our fight, and not to use up ammo, because PK was hit so often they could not give us ammo. Right in front of me, men were shot and then carried away as a blood trail was visible I could hear on the radio "man down", while this was going on in front of me. My truck's left back tire was blown out. When silence returned, I changed it.

5e
War has its price, a heavy mind

May 2011

My first real firefight was right after we left Alpha's OP, PK, folks were shooting at us, and we shot back. The fight ended badly. Both Charlie company and Alpha's quick reaction force had to help us. One of Alpha's guys ended up being shot right in front of me and Green. We saw him fall and be dragged away. I saw his face was in shock. My squad leader Sgt Salcedo was shot, one of our gunners ended up getting hit (Gallow) too, and our battalion colonel was hit as well, but his plate vest shattered, and he walked away ok. I fought with myself, as if to put my kindness in a cage for the time being and become sharp aggressive as tracers were flying just above our truck. I could hear the bullets twist while cutting the air. Night came, and our team was left alone to drive back to OP Bostic. It was a quiet drive, alone with my gunner Green, while Sgt Salcedo seat was empty.

I held my eyes low, my chest felt tight. Our guys made it okay, but I felt fear for the first time, and it was bitter, and dark, something movies, or games try to mimic, and there I was driving back, with an empty seat. Fear followed me, and in the nights, it kept me awake.

<u>5f</u>

Blurred vision of perpetual
failure the two of me fight
for inner space.

May 2011

The night we got back, our team leaders gave us a small talk, that this summer would be very busy for us, that since we didn't have a company, we would be working alongside any company that needed us, while also doing our own job, person security detachment, but then I heard a commotion, and I ran out of the barracks. The first Americans had hit an IED. I heard the name Blevins from Alpha, so I ran fast as I could to the medic room, where they were asking for volunteers to carry the men. *I knew Blevins. He was in my platoon in basic,* I said, and they allowed my squad to carry him.

We stood over the four bodies, blood everywhere, and I felt dread for the first time. The smell of burnt clothing and flesh was very strong. I kept my eye on Cain (who was in first squad), not wanting to look down. We walked with the bodies out into the night and to the choppers, glow sticks lighting our way, as flares were shot way up in the sky, to say goodbye. The choppers left, and I kept standing there until someone grabbed me and pulled me away. I walked away still watching the helicopter fly in to the dark, and this moment found it self in my dreams.

4b

I looked past the night, and

there the

war lit the sky,

and through my eyes light

covered my sight until

day and night were one.

The shadows of the night

shown

my shadow, and smoke

touched the clouds.

This memory hunts me, as us

six carried one.

May 2011

A few days passed. While my team was doing inventory, making sure everything was squared away, another death was announced. This time it was a few Afghan soldiers. I stood near my barracks, looking. They put the bodies on the choppers, then left, and it was quiet again. Walking back to the barracks, I could see our team having fun, laughing and joking. We ate together, showered together, and talked together about anything. Then I saw it, I was just like them, folks trying to have a better life, and this was our ticket. Most had never gone to college, nor wanted to. But they did want a better life, so, this was it. If they could make it back home, they could use this experience to find a good job, or use the GI Bill to pay for school, or to learn a trade skill. I saw that each of their eyes held hope, and when they smiled it made me smile too. I also saw their worry and fear. I saw that I was just like them. I was no better, no smarter, just a soul doing what it took to find happiness. But, when one soul is taken away, we forever keep them in our minds, and put one foot in front of the other, and keep going, something that was hard for me to do.

5g

I can see the coglike
structure to life.
If one wheel is taken out,
another will fall in to its
place. But I am
no shape which fits in this
thing.

May 2011

Chapter Three

Lost Youth

Every morning, mortar rounds came in. We got used to them. Our beds would shake a little, then we would hear the rocks fall back down around our little barracks. My stomach would feel as though it dropped, and I would jump off my bed, and sit low to the ground, and as the next round came in the sound was like a falling ambulance. There was this high-pitched scream as it got closer to the ground, then a high-pitched explosion that was followed with a deep grumble sound, then an echo bounced round the valley, then the sound came back again, but lower then lower then lower until the next round would come in. The time between each round was about 30 seconds, from the time they shot it to the time it landed. So after the first explosion, you knew you had half a minute to hide or move to the next spot before getting down again. The incoming had me very jumpy, for obvious reasons, but that forced me to overreact one morning, and I slipped off my truck and fractured my left ankle, The burning pain taught me to control my fears.

<u>4c</u>

The random chaotic angles
of life
have no one perspective.

June 2011

Summer came, and with it came war. Every moment my platoon was on the move, we were always shooting something. There were times when we did not have a chance to sleep for days, and other times when some of us just could not sleep though we tried. We would wake up to incoming bombs. Most learned to just rolled over and fall back to sleep, but I looked at the ceiling and wondered if a round would come through and hit me. Sometimes in the mornings you could hear the rounds smash a sleeping quarters, and feel the ground shake, and then yelling and screaming followed._I sometimes would get up, and I could see everyone's eyes looking at the ceiling, too. Then someone would clear their throat trying to swallow their fear. You could hear their throat tighten as they tried to swallow. Nothing we could do. Some would get up and make some coffee. Me, I just put on music, something from Jonny Cash. I had his music on my iPod, and I would close my eyes, and try to dream of being somewhere else. I watched Rowe, Savoy, and Ruble line up, and run out one morning, just to get breakfast..... war and chaos became our norm....

<u>5h</u>

Knowledge, I believe
will set the mind free
from agony.

June 2011

These days, we jumped around to PK, Alpha's OP, the Afghan police checkpoint, and Bravo's OP. The nights were not quiet, and like gladiators we fought. How strange it was, that I was hunting other humans that were hunting me. I felt like a mouse hiding from a cat or an owl. Combat and violence brushed against us each moment. Any wrong steps or mistakes were met with pain, agony, and sometimes death. Being nervous was part of my days. One warm day, black smoke blocked out the sun, I leaned against a trench-like wall at PK, looking up at the smoke and tracers while men ran back and forth: I was waiting for food in line, I watched Bluhm running in to get a few bites of food, then run back to shoot more rounds off.

One morning at PK, bombs woke us up. My team lined up. We could see the rounds hitting everywhere. I was first in line and Cain was second, and my time was up: "GO!" With all my gear, I ran through everything, pushing my way to our trucks. I felt as if I was stuck in a nightmare, running in slow motion past the rounds and bouncing tracers. I made it, but it was like this every day, and this nightmare was real. I could not awaken.

5i

I have such a long way,
in the short
time given.

June 2011

My team, the Omen Element, fought alongside with every company. We helped Charlie when they needed us, we seemed to live in between Monti and PK, and we were put on quick reaction force for just about permanent at Nishgon police station.

The fighting started about 2pm on this day. It was one big move for the enemy. All at once they hit each AO and my team was right in the middle. Throughout the day, we saw explosions on all sides of the hills and mountains. As each hour passed it felt as though it was going to get really bad. SSG Gibson told us to get in our trucks and lock the doors. As the sun fell, the fighting started to intensify. I was on the gun, and we had to put our night vision on, and through the night explosions and tracers were everywhere. We had to bomb every hill and mountain. There was fire all around us. As fighting went on, I broke my night vision, and I could not see well, as fear filled me I saw the bright red rounds and bright white explosions that lit the night. I was asked to laser each spot of enemy fire with our Crow system (a type of rocket).

<u>4d</u>

I the one in the cage
of conditioning can't
find the key.
This repeat is
now annoying.

June 2011

We lazed the enemy position, and saw rounds smash the mountains. Apachies flew throughout the Valley, just waiting to get a chance to blow up the enemy. The mountains around us flashed in sets, bright white explosion was followed with deep thundering sounds. Throughout the night tracers were traded in every which direction I could see SSG Gibson and Ruble running to each truck, as our radios kept getting static. Moments of pure light made the night day, just for a second as the shock wave rumbled our trucks.

About 5am, the fighting stopped. Then just like that there was a pause, a moment of quietness. There was still radio chatter. As I stood on my gunners seat, Baker handed me a lit cigarette. I took off my headset to listen. There was no bird chirp, or any dog bark, or anything. Where there were trees, now lay burnt embers. I could hear CSM Manis's voice. It was calm and clear. *I guess some people are made for this,* I thought while I looked at the scars left on the earth and fire across the valley from the battle that night. I always thought this valley was so beautiful, but it was also hell. So I guess it was the beauty of war.

<u>4e</u>

The congested mind

over fills and

spills into my dreams.

June 2011

Our battalion used our cooks, our mechanics, our drivers, anyone that we could find, to help fight. I saw the people that weren't infantry helping us at Alpha's forward operating base, like our cooks who made food, or our mechanics shooting up the mountains. They had signed up to cook food or fix trucks, but ended up trying not to get shot. I saw women shooting too, and running around with ammo. If we got lucky, my team would guard the prisoners and protect our translators. There was one women who took a liking to me, maybe because I was brown. Her job was to translate. My job was to keep her alive. On July fourth, OP Bostic celebrated our freedom, my team shot hand flares up, and we smiled and laughed. The following morning, my team was looking at 28 dead Afghan soldiers who died in the night from a raid north of Bostic. I sat, looking at the mingled bodies, twisted, and red, Sgt Labonty tapped my shoulder, holding chew tobacco. I took a big pinch, as the morning sun shined bright over the dead, bodies. I saw it in each of our guys, it felt as if our youth was fading away.

<u>5i</u>

The passing smiles, the

"just missed,"

the frown, the fear,

a flash and the

morning calm broken

by a

bomb.

July 2011

At PK, Alpha's OP, doing my watch at night. With my night vision I could see rounds being traded, it lasted until morning, I was with SGT Labonty running around PK trying to not stay in one spot too long. When dust next to him was popped, he looked at me and said, "Was that for me?" I looked at him and answered, "No." Then he laughed. My team goal was to ensure the safety of the next resupply when it came by but that night my best pal and his staff sergeant were killed. While in PK's chow room where we waited, I could hear it on the radio. "Black out... black out... US troops hit, and down...... Bravo 1st platoon... SGT James Christen dead... SGT Jacob Molina dead... wounded are on route..." I sat, listening to the radio chatter. I was sad and wanted to cry, but the resupply was coming our way, and should be with us at morning, and I remember I curled up next to my battle buddy Green, trying to sleep, but I could only hear the chatter and combat. I just wanted to hide, but there was nowhere I could. I had to bite my lip and make sure I was ready for the morning.

4f

The history of man has

led me

here,

and the weight of it burns

my soul

July 2011

The morning sun shined bright as I got in to my truck. I helped my gunner for the day, who was a great pal of mine. My stomach dropped when I saw the black smoke rise way up to the sky in the direction where we were headed Sgt Bluhm came over "alright, lets do the job we singed up for" he said, looking up at the black clouds.

That morning my team was placed on the side of a mountain, stuck, forced to fight, in our trucks. Rivers of flames ran down the hills as the resupply was hit, and the fuel trucks pored gas, fire everywhere. To our left was the face of a mountain, and to our right was at least a hundred foot drop, and there was only enough room for one truck to move in one direction.

My gunner was shooting for hours when our 50 cal jammed, and he had to get on top of the truck to fix the barrel. My gunner said to me, "If I get hit, please pull me back in." I looked at Sgt Labonty. He nodded while taking shots from his seat. My gunner stood on our truck trying to readjust the 50 cal, and my sergeant stood out his door shooting, I was on the radio doing my best to relaying information, I only opened the door when it was needed.

<u>4g</u>

Remember... even in the

front lines...

one who hides...

will need to face his

fears.... You can't

hide from what

needs crossing over.

July 2011

While helping my gunner, I had my door open, when BOOM, the mountain wall to our left was hit by something. I closed my door. Our other trucks took their turns shooting rockets back. I watched Holland run to the trucks on fire he saw each car were filled with dead men then he went back to his truck and pushed off the vehicles over the cliff which were on fire to our right and blocking our way. Each second passed felt so slow. Another explosion, another bellow of fire, another fuel truck was hit, and the fuel fell from the cliff into the river creating a literal river of fire. Each truck went forward because we were at the point were no truck was able to turn around. We were stuck and there was only one way, which was through, through the fight, and through the fire and past our fears, and each foot we gained was gained through violence. Then another truck was pushed off the cliff into the river of fire by lead truck who was Savoy and Holland. The black smoke tilted toward us, and the sun was blocked out. I started to hear over our platoon radio that our guys were getting very low on ammo. Noon came, and we each took our turn eating our MREs.

4h

Socrates was right.

Shadows and chains.

July 2011

After about 3pm we were still stuck getting hit from every direction. Then I saw SSG Gibson jump out of his truck and run to each of our trucks, asking for all our smoke grenades, which we gave him. We saw him walk in front of our trucks, all by himself, and threw the smoke grenades, everyone shot from their truck, Rowe shot and killed a enemy close range just across the river. All the shooting stopped. Then in a flash a few Apache came to our rescue, and our trucks were able to push forward. We passed by the trucks that had been on fire, some still burning and others just smoke and melted to the road. While passing them, I did not even try to look into them. I did not want to see the burnt dead.

We got back that evening, and that night we did not sleep. We had to fuel up and get what we needed, and we were off again. We drove through the night, and as we passed back through same area, we saw that the trucks weren't on fire anymore, but there was a small flame in a few trucks that burned throughout the night like lanterns in the night. It felt strange to see them burn in the far distance, knowing there lay dead men.

5k

In the dark
your goals
will light your way

July 2011

Chapter Four
Fall and Winter

This cool morning, I was on the ground and next to me was Baker. We both ducked, and above us was smoke from a mortar round explosion. I thought to myself, *how did I end up here?* The molten metal hit everything around me and Baker. I was on my stomach when he got up and grabbed my shirt, pulling me up, and I took a deep breath while rocks fell back down around us. The echo of the round still ringing in my ear. I could hear the crunching sound of dirt as we ran. We left our trucks behind, they were stuck in line at the test-firing pit, due to the first truck's engine being blown out. Baker and I made it back, but Straten (our radio guy) was still in one of the trucks doing radio check. Our team leader asked, would someone go and give him his gear? I raised my hand and ran back to the truck. Once I got there, I heard a round coming in, so I jumped under the truck he was in. But when the round landed a few meters away, it didn't go off. I could hear the crackling and sizzling sound of the round still burning, like an egg on a hot frying pan.

<u>51</u>

Self destruction seems to

be

a part of me,

I can't stop this random

chaotic

style of life,

that I found myself in.

The door won't open

stuck to face my

doings.

August 2011

In August, we had one last resupply before the cold came. Our goal was to first go to Monti, pick up new trucks, and then drive with the supplies back to Bostic, which was about a two-day trip. We brought the media, like CNN, with us to take them around our area, driving them to each OP so they could take pictures and hang out with the men.

On our first night, we stopped at an area called Gooey Ridge and spent the night there. Once the morning came, we were ambushed. The truck behind me was hit, and I saw flames and smoke. Then my truck was hit, which made it lift off the ground a little, and the explosion shook my head. I was ordered to shoot anyone on the mountains that were to our left, using our truck gun system. I turned it to White Hot, which means anything warm would be white and everything else was black. I saw two hot signals 900 meters to our rear. I zeroed in, and shot. Each round that landed had those areas splashed with bright white. My 50 cal was running low, and my driver, without thinking twice, jumped on my truck to help me, Savoy came to my door, and took my M48 to help push back the ambush.

<u>3a</u>

Learn to accept structured Chaos

August 2011

We blew up the whole mountain. CSM Manis, yelling on the radio as I watched Ruble trying not to get hit while trying to shoot back, I was shooting the 50 cal and saw the rounds hit all around him. The whole side of the mountain exploded from a number of 155s. Kerstan jumped on my truck to fill my rounds. I watched him, as chaos held his hand, smoke everywhere, the ground shaking, and there he was with a cigarette in his mouth loading my gun. He even had time to take one last hit from it then flick it before putting in the last round.

We drove through the night to Monti. CSM Manis was in the passenger seat talking of his younger days, and every now and then I would tease him. "Hey you guys know any good songs?" he asked, while the gun wobbled back and forth making metallic sounds as the truck bounced around. I answered "I have that one song you like on my iPod." He looked back with a smile and said "Really?" I smiled and said, "Of course not, Sergeant Major Manis." Then everyone started laughing, he mumble bad words, but he laughed too.

5m

Today I've
seen the smiles
of sorrow

August 2011

My birthday came, and I said nothing, maybe because I talked too much, or maybe I just didn't want to bother anyone. I sat doing tower duty, remembering my pals. Thinking that I was a kid playing tag with my friends, and then, in another moment, I was carrying a friend in a body bag, loading him into a chopper. My mind kept jumping around. I smoked a cig, thinking of this, then that.

By this time, I had forgotten what home was like, so I kept reading, and writing, hiding my past in books. Something in me just gave up. I was tired of being afraid, but moments forced me to stay afraid.

After tower duty I went to our sleeping quarters to sleep, but once I finally fell asleep, a mortar round came in through the ceiling and blew up the blast wave shook our beds and metal flew everywhere. I was dragged off my bed by Kersten. Through the commotion and confusion it was the screaming that fully woke me. I grabbed my gear, and while I put it on, I heard another explosion. I stood low and then walked through the smoke. I walked because there was nowhere to run, our sleeping quarters were the safest place.

3b

The friction of time wears

on me

September 29 2011

Charlie's guys were being pulled out. I sat in the doorway, smoke behind me, when I saw SSG Gibson looking at me. He gave a motion to say, "Clip your chin strap," and I did. To my right men were helping the wounded. They were trying to stop the bleeding. I looked down, bit my lip, the smell of the round was in my mouth, and I spit trying to get rid of the bad flavor.

My team leader Labonty walked with Bluhm past me, then he stopped, popped a cigarette in his mouth, and pulled me up to stand. They both looked at me and asked "Are you hurt?" I nodded to say I am ok, then both of them walked to the next guy in our squad and did the same. I spaced out and thought to remember: what was home like? I used to smoke weed before swim class, then smoke weed again before art class. The flavor of the round was still in my nose. While I tried to blow it out, Sgt Labonty came back to me and said, "Hey you get your shit ready, we're getting breakfast." I gave a nod and made sure to put away my M48 and get my M4. At breakfast I had eggs, and a lot of potatoes.

4i

In to the nothing, a ways

and

far from home.

here the sounds of

loneliness

have become too loud.

September 2011

The morning cold had arrived, and Baker and I got into an argument. He was going to get my truck weapons up and ready, and I was going to do his, but he wanted me to do his radio check also, which I felt I did not have to do. I stood on his truck, getting the m240 ready, putting things in their right place, when I heard a WAMP sound and shouting. I looked up and saw everyone running. I just had enough time to jump off the truck when a round hit ten feet from me. It cut a seven-foot-tall Hesco in half. I fell to my knees, smoke and dust everywhere. My head was hurting, and I saw colors everywhere I looked, but I managed to pull myself to the driver's seat of Baker's truck and close the door. Tears ran down my face and my chest was hurting from the explosion, so I did the only thing I could think of: put my headphones on and listen to Jonny Cash's "I walk the line." I closed my eyes, and thought of the salty waves of Hawaii. I remembered the warm ocean, and all the smiles that played in the water with me. My head felt like a knife was stuck in it and the pain went away slowly.

3c

I find myself in a story,

the words on the page

are my life,

and

like the beginning,

this story has an end.

October 2011

While working with the Afghan police force I had to walk to my truck for guard duty, and coming toward me was a kid in a blue outfit. I thought nothing of it. But I looked in to his eyes and saw such sadness and hate and loss, his eyes were so distressful, I stopped in my tracks and smiled at him. But he just looked away. That night we got back to our sleeping quarters, and over the radio we got word that the very same Afghan police checkpoint where we had been helping out was blown up by a young boy who simply walked in. I can't say if this young boy was the same one I saw, but I can say that we spent the next five months working with the police force there after the event and I never saw that kid again.

These days felt as if every moment I was ending on a bad note all the time. It was both sour and bitter. Nothing I did made it go away.

I stopped looking people in the eye, and I felt broken. That young guy who loved making others happy was lost. I stopped trying too.

5n

The walking end is such a

beautiful thing,

the master piece of

happiness is being created

November 2011

Fall came, and cool winds blew our way. The fighting slowed down. This gave me time to relax a little, and continue my writings and artwork. When we went out, we did not worry so much, as fighting became a normal part of our day. When rounds came in, we shot back, and did not panic any longer. We knew what to do, and we did it well. Winter came, the fighting was very slow. But we did have to worry about snipers and IEDs. My team almost ran over an IED. By luck we stopped. The enemy blew it up anyway. I saw molten metal fly as high as the mountains around us when it blew. The night was covered in light as the red hot metal fell back to the earth, the bright white red flames were like a glimpse into hell. I drew again, but I learned not to show the Afghan people my modern abstract art, as a man had pulled a gun on me for showing it to him. We got used to sleeping and working with the Afghan police. When we slept with the Afghan forces, we had one guy pointing a gun out the door while we slept. Soldiers had died for trusting too much. We made sure not to follow those steps.

<u>4i</u>

I am lost in any direction,

and in every way,

my self has grown numb.

November 2011

I left home for my two-week vacation on December 24th. I was the last of my team to take a vacation. The reason I wanted to do that was to be there every moment of the war, so when I left for home, it was snowy, no more fighting, and I didn't have to feel guilty leaving my guys. Home for two weeks felt like a dream—fuzzy and unfocused. It passed by fast.

Everyone grew a little, and I grew a little, too, but I grew apart from my family and the life I once knew. When I got back to Afghanistan, I was stuck in Jalalabad, and I stayed there for a month due to snow. I enjoyed it. I saw movies and drank coffee and talked with other soldiers from different countries—Germany, France, and Great Britain—I listened to their stories about their homes and families and battles. I sat with some random guys one cold and black night and we laughed. I could see that each person wanted the same thing. A better tomorrow. They wanted to be happy. I felt horrible when I found out the Charlie medic was killed the day I left home. Even still I think how sad it must be for his family.

3d

The echo of war haunts me

December 2011

Chapter Five
The Start of Our Lives

My last year in the military went fast. I took college courses, and I kept doing art. I went to the clubs, and had fun. I was asked if I wanted to stay in, and I really thought about it, but I felt as though I had done my part, and for me it was over. So I didn't sign up for more years.

I was moved to S-3, which was helping with events and keeping track of what each company was doing so we could go with them and help them set up. Because I had studied art before I joined the military, they made me the battalion photographer, and I always got great photos, mostly because I staged what was going on. One time, I had some Charlie company guys run in front of the camera while I threw some leftover 5.56 bullet cases at them. It looked epic, as if they were in intense training. My pictures were selected to be used in *Army Times*, or websites, or whatever they thought would be fit to make the Army look good or the 25th division, a handful of times.

<u>3e</u>

My mind, even though
lost, has its moments
of pure bliss.

April 2012

There was one time a group of guys were just waiting around, and I asked them to act as if they were planning something. Some drew on the ground, others pointed in random directions. Everyone laughed at me, but once they saw my photo was picked, they always listened to my ideas. Finally my time was up, and I had a one-way ticket to go back home. I cleaned out my room and said bye.

I thought all of it was over, but the war seemed not to be done with me. Us few take on a task, which most will never know, and I was the few, I learned so much, and I was thankful for the new family that I gained, but really? Who was I? just a kid, a kid like us all. I guess this is when the story gets real.

I kept writing in my journal, I kept writing poems and quotes to help share what was going on, to put together what life was for me. I left Hawaii, and a few hours later, I was home. I felt good at first. I was going to college, and doing art again. I felt great. But the honeymoon slipped by, and I woke up, I got back to my hometown in late spring 2013.

3f

The contradictions of life

and thought

are only a part

of the

aging mind.

July 2012

Back in Fresno, I was too busy with how strong I was and the money I had saved up. I broke from my family, and lost track of them. Like the same side of magnets, we pushed away. We no longer lived in the same reality, though I was being pulled back into it. A few days back home, I was staying at my sister's, drunk and happy, and my mother was about to come to visit. I was so proud of myself, a war hero, a college boy, her boy. When she came in, she was high on crack, skinny, and she had brought another skinny crackhead with her. She didn't even notice her baby boy. I was a shadow to her. She looked around my sister's apartment for loose change.

Then I remembered what I was running from. I got up, went to my wallet and pulled money out, gave it to my mom, and she was gone. I held the door as she walked away. Who was I? Nothing. I came from nothing, and I was nothing. I sat alone, doing art, when sadness found me again. A soul raised in destruction, who went to war hoping that would fix a broken home, only came back to misery.

4k

Total destruction is the

foundation

to one's road to *"peace."*

2013

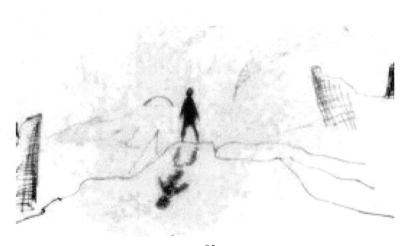

Chapter Six
Philosophy of This Life

Sitting with liquor, sadness seemed to always find me, drinking through the night, watching the stars move across the night sky with a tilt. I would drink sitting outside until the sun came up. Then, I would take a shower, and go to my college classes. I sat in class with a beard, still drunk. I saw these young kids in college doing art next to me. They smiled, and joked, and some missed class. Some had just turned 18.

School, life, and how I used to live meant nothing any longer to me. Something in me broke. We don't get to choose our family, or our start in life, so I decided to choose how this life of mine would end. There was so much I did not know, and this was the first time I could see that I knew nothing. By switching my arts major to philosophy, I stepped away from everything I knew once more, trying to escape the war that was like a throne in my mind escape the path given to me.

Only through self-realization and philosophy did I overcome the absence in my life.

<u>3g</u>

Being new to everything,

only proves to me that

I am but a child in the

eyes of time.

May 2013

This was the first time I dropped acid, and it changed everything. While seeing folks dancing and chatting, I saw that my drive for an adventure was not done. Being alive is hard, when we have limits around us, keeping us in our place, yet we are raised to think that we can do anything we dream of. Then we grow up and see that the bounderies are visible in the neighborhoods we are raised in, in the level of education we are able to achieve, and in the life we are given. Leaving my home was not a hard choice. I left with a one way ticket to Asia, not knowing what would happen.

Sometimes one needs to keep going. We don't really know why our thoughts come about, but there is something in us, and it wants something. Something that is hard to see when our world blinds us. Our lives are broken into pieces—family, friends, work, fun, and so on—and each institution has its own way of seeing things, rules, and ways to act. Maybe the war that I went through broke my lens to life, but something was different.

4l

The ripples of a
meaningless thought have
reached the end.

June 2014

Carl Jung showed me that this life is built with structures, and I was on the bottom. The ladder was real, I could see it in Asia. I saw it because I stood outside of their social reality.

Social constructionist helped me understand what class was, and how each group stays in their circle. I sat one night drinking with some random Chinese guys, and one of them said something to me that I had heard my whole life: "a real man works with his hands." The man showed me his rough hands, and was proud of them. Then, a few weeks later, I drank with a successful business guy, we talked, and he said something similar: "a real man uses his head to make money." We got drunk and laughed. For me, I saw that no matter where each of those men stood in life, they, like me, were going in one direction, and that was death. For me, society was death's waiting room.

So I saw life as a ride. We live this life and pass what we created to the next generation, in hope that the next generation will do it better than we did. And I saw I could not get off.

2a

I can't get off this one-way
ride, this life is
more bizarre than
my mind can ever
understand.

2014

Emile Durkheim taught me that suffering comes from the very society that you come from: social pathology. We cast addicts away, but never look at what causes it all. We blame the dead for their own suicide.

What we are is the very thing that we come from. We can't hide how our minds are made. Those who teach us what life is and the rules to it put us on a road that is very hard to leave. Without answers, what could I say that others did not already know? But something was in them that kept them in their world, something kept them in their suffering.

While painting, I would watch the sun fall, then rise. I saw that not only did I have no say in my reality, I had no say in this world. It spun, and each morning the world woke up and kept busy until night came.

I learned that I knew nothing. No matter how much I read, no answers came, only more questions. I kept painting, and reading, and I drank too much and too often, as the war kept creeping in my dreams.

2b

Today I want to study

something

"*strange*," but I don't want

to know "*me...*"

so I will do nothing

today....

2014

Alan Watts taught me that this life is a game, and I play it because it is I who made it.

Living on the outside of society in China, I saw the games that people play. There is no real anything. We create titles, then place them on people. Those titles are given to us through merit or are forced on us, and they tell others how to treat us. And I saw, that I did not choose my race, my skin color, my name, nor where I was born, yet I am forever stuck with these titles. I finally understood what double consciousness was, and how I would have to live with these titles.

I was playing the game, whether I liked it or not. I was ranked by other people, and I was judged by them, too. As I walked the streets of China and partied every weekend, I saw people just like me, trying to live and make the best out of being alive, while trying to play this game called life. I saw that I was playing this game with everyone else, and each knew something that I didn't.

3h

I am a fool playing

a game among

Intellects.

2015

For what reason is it that life wants to live?, and why is it that life needs us to live through its creations? It feels as if this body is our prison, and society is our cage. We must live through each moment, and who we are is built memory. Our behavior is a collection of mistakes. And our world only feels as if it is outside of our head.

These rule we live by have me chained to them. I can see now that I never had real free will, and that I have always been a cog in this giant thing, and being way down at the bottom, there was so much to look at down here. I wonder why anyone would bring life into being just to see them suffer. Maybe because they had no choice? Or maybe they were just experiencing this reality and going through the motions of being alive. The rules tell them to find love and create more humans.

I see the world differently now. Social philosophy woke my soul up. How sad I was to finally be awake, with my time closer to my end.

<u>2c</u>

The *"whys"* in human life
never end.
They linger
like an awkward echo.

2015

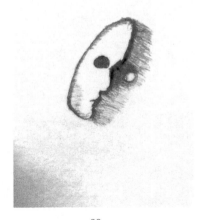

Chapter Seven
Stuck in the Rabbit Hole

Michel Foucault, Ludwig Wittgenstein and others taught me the rules of life, not because they are right or wrong, but because that is what was taught to those before us. Everything became meaningless to me. I painted and did art each day to keep me from thinking too much. But then I asked my own mortality: For what is it that I must play this game? My emotions dictated my actions, and the "I" who I thought I was only a being that came to life by two other humans who also came the same way, and I was not special. My thoughts were out of my control, yet my needs forced me to drink and eat and gravitate toward sex. And still, I, the one looking through the eyes of this body, was the one who had to experience each moment. If my body was in pain, then I was the one who felt it, and this body was named "Abel." I was assigned a sound for a name, and given numbers like a farm animal, which is my SSN. I saw it: I was a sheep with a tag that broke free from the line. It is true, with knowledge comes power, but with true knowledge comes suffering.

<u>3i</u>

Our memory is the only
thing we can
trust. Until we gain
knowledge, then do we
realize that our life is
meaningless.

2015

Sitting looking out a window overlooking the city of Shenzhen, I could see how life worked itself out to make this thing, to make society. And I could see that no matter how much I learned the rules, it did me no good. I could not use this knowledge for gain, so I decided to put the answer to our lives in my art, and give them away.

My goal was to touch the heart of whatever this is, which I am a part of. I wanted to try to reach the heart of life. So, like all thinkers and philosophers, I wrote the answer to life not in a book, but first I wrote it on my paintings, which by now I had done about a hundred, and they were traveling who knows where. I could see that people are smart enough to pay the rent, or take care of their loved ones, but they were like me. We do not have the mind to understand what this thing is, what we are living through. It looks to me like life and humans are both different and connected, humans want to live, but life itself does not need humans for it to keep going. Maybe we are a mistake created by nature, or we are the universe waking up.

<u>2d</u>

I am a fool with
knowledge,
able to see the heart of
society, but
I am unable to touch it.

2015

Nietzsche taught me what love was, which was out of my control. I was a slave for my emotions and lust. I loved it when I could hold this young woman, and listen to her days. She just finished college, she was very shy., and when she cried, I held her. I would say in those moments "*I will always be here.*" Whatever she wanted I did my best to get, and at night, I would always make sure to put my artwork second to her. She would come home from work, and I would stop whatever I was doing. One early morning, I was eating breakfast with her, her black hair pulled back, her cheeks pink, and red lips had me stuck staring at her. She fed me while we sat close. I said nothing, and I listened to her. She had on a white blouse, and a dark blue skirt that hugged her thin waist, and when her bangs fell over her eyes, I brushed it back behind her ear. So Nietzsche was right, I loved this young women because I was selfish. Nothing I could do, to escape being a human, so I fell in love.

<u>1a</u>

How strange, I stare in the

eyes of love,

and

love stares back.

2015

One morning, while my queen was getting ready for work, I was in my art room, drunk, and had not slept for two days and nights. She came to give me a kiss, and I saw it, I saw her sadness toward me. She could not look me in the eye. I tried to kiss her hands, but she pulled away, then she left to work. I was a drunk, with nothing to give to her. If she was with me, she would have to work. My heart dropped. My past, which I didn't agree to be part of, was now shining bright. I had no family for her to visit, no father, mother, or even aunts or uncles. I sat in my room for days. We grew apart. She would leave for a few days for her work. I think these are the times she could breathe. This is around the time I came to understand that I had PTSD, and what it was. The war stuck in my mind and destroyed my world. The me that was a school guy and an artist was lost. And this is the time I had to try anything to be me again. I went to the war to have more schooling, but I left stuck in dreams of combat, dreams of screams. I now know — I never slept just so I would not dream.

2e

The rewards my body
gives to me, make
me a slave to
society.

2016

Looking out of my art room, watching the sun fall, I could feel the warm spring winds blow into the room. I sat drinking red wine and it made my jaw clinch a little from the sourness. My thoughts bounced around like a broken record set on a sad song. The apartment was empty. There was something in me, something sad, and that sadness floated to the top of my mind each time the sun rose. I felt a tightness in my chest, and some days I could not breathe. The war stayed very clear in my mind. When I could go to sleep, I would wake, and stay awake. I would not trust anyone. I had to change this environment, and I had to find a way to free my self from me, from my past. So when my queen came back from her two-week business trip, I showed her the artwork and told her my new plan. I would pull out all of my stocks, and we would move to her family's hometown in central China and start our own school. With a smile, she agreed, wiping her tears away. Just like that, we packed up, got the finished work into the University of Shenzhen, and left for Hunan.

<u>3j</u>

Alone, and the sounds

that come with it

are all around.

2016

I never stopped having my art goals, but now, I would use everything that I had learned, and was learning, to start a school from scratch. She was the teacher, and I did everything else.

We live this life, and from moment to moment it feels as though the life we live is new to us, but us as a group have been doing what we have since the start of man. Each of us goes through the same things. We age, learn, work, love, and we hope what we do makes us happy.

We are copies of copies, and there I was in a new reality, everyone looking at me, the only non-Chinese, a guy with a beard. And we did it from scratch. We built a small school, starting with 5 students, and by the end of the summer we had 40 students. I still found myself drinking too much, and the sadness of the war found me late in the night. I could not shake it, and I knew there were others like me struggling to keep these thoughts of the war from showing, struggling to hold on to a smile. I felt as though I was walking in circles, repeating the very things I wanted to let go.

<u>2f</u>

My un-repeated steps are

new to the world,

but irony finds

me riding

the same roads

2016

I flew back to my hometown, and gave gifts out. I went to see my brother and my sister. The first day was fun, but the next, I sat next to my brother while we watched tv. He couldn't work because he was a felon and known gang member. He just waited until night to party. And my sister worked so often. My news of opening a school in Asia and getting married slipped by them. My mother was on the streets. I went to see her. She was living in a tent next to a highway close to a hotel on the 99 and Golden State. Nothing that I had learned, not from any of the books, none of the deep philosophical ideas, allowed me to put words together to say anything to my mother. I saw her eyes, and there was no soul. She had six random dogs with her, and she could not stop moving around, picking up one dog then another. What kind of son am I? I was so busy trying to make others proud of me when I should have been doing what I could to help my mother. I did one thing, before saying bye. I gave her money, and I saw her walk away again.

<u>1b</u>

Through all the moments

who I wish to be.

I find myself trapped,

in the very thing

which I hate to

be.

2016

Before I left to go back to Asia, I went to a music festival where I took acid, I was happy, danced for hours, and laughed with my night friends, but thoughts of my mother stayed with me. After seeing my mother like that, I wanted to understand why so, knowing an old friend of mine, I thought to talk with him, and try the hardest drug could get.

I ended up with meth, something my mother did, and I finely got it. I understood why she did what she did, and why she left her family. As a kid I could only blame her, and hate that she was never there, but now, myself looking through the eyes of a meth head, I saw it, and I was dragged deeper than I ever wanted to go. I felt what addiction really was, and my reality was destroyed. I stood at the edge of sanity, and jumped off. My thinking changed, and my goals shifted toward the high and stayed there. I wanted to go through her pain, and understand what a broken dream feels like, and I did. It was like shattered glass flowing through my heart. My smiles were hollow that filled with sadness and hate.

1c

We surround our self's
with others, but lonely
always finds us.

August 2016

I found myself in a hotel room, smoking with my new pals. Each had his own pipe, like me. And after a month, I ended up hooked. I could not stop, I spent hundreds and lost over 30lbs. Sitting there, watching my iPad, a person tapping my shoulder to give me a hit, while smoking I had a moment of clarity and I saw it: I saw pain. I looked around. These people only had each other, and on each face I saw agony, so I stood up, as their eyes watched me, I gave my bag to my old pal, and I said good bye, and left.

The crash was very bad. I could not eat, I could not see straight, and I was hearing voices from everywhere. I got a text from my wife, then I sat down in one spot and let the wave of pure pain clean me up. My love for my queen was stronger than the addiction I had created. I sat there for days sweating and keeping calm while shaking. I finally became clean, and the next day, I bought my ticket to China. When I held my love, I was happy. In the dark we lay and she played on her phone. I stared at her. I finally knew what love was. I bit my lip, holding it all in. I hugged her close, and fell asleep.

<u>2g</u>

From a dream I wake,

my open eyes can see

that "me", has fallen

in to a nightmare.

The taste of agony is

everywhere.

May 2017

Jordan Peterson taught me that it is okay to say goodbye and how to overcome obstacles placed by others and how to defeat my dragons.

I can't say my journey was easy. I did not choose to be born. I did not choose my name, nor my race. Yet I am stuck with these titles. I see my face age, and that my past is stuck with me. This book was about my twenties, and I like to think of me as those characters from movies, the one that walks away in the far distance as it rains while the credits roll up, and the viewers wonder whatever happened to him. I don't know either, but I will leave on a good note, I smile much more now, and each morning, I kiss my wife to wake her up. My life is not perfect, and I still drink too much, but I gave my wife a school. She is happy, which makes me happy. I have much more time to do art and writing, our school is doing well with over 100 students, a few teachers, and an assistant. Something about the war has opened my eyes up. It made me try harder for what I believe in, and to never give up in situations that I once thought were too hard.

<u>1d</u>

Passing from moment

to moment, being a part

of this thing called

life and *society*,

no knowledge,

or set of words,

can ever stop the

hand of *time*.

Day by day,

I watch my *turn* in line,

to take part in the grand scheme

of it all.

2018

We live this life, and hope that what we do today will ripple into our future, creating the dreams we hope to have. This life is best lived with others, even though the others make it difficult. If life is too easy, we get bored. But if life is too hard, we give up and quit. Our lives are best when we struggle just enough to get what we want. Thus, we need others in our lives to help us make those dreams come true. I could not be a writer if not for the readers, I could not be an artist if not for art lovers, and I could not be loved if not for my wife. We don't know what life is, but we know it is something we are placed in, and this ride is best when we are riding with everyone else.

The fall through life is a short one, let us fall together.

<u>0a</u>

"Free will and something

else."

The epic of life

is meaningless

without "you........."

2018

125

127

Made in United States
North Haven, CT
28 February 2022

16606530R00075